SOOT

poems by

Joe Betz

Finishing Line Press
Georgetown, Kentucky

SOOT

Copyright © 2023 by Joe Betz
ISBN 979-8-88838-136-6 First Edition
All rights reserved under International and Pan-American Copyright Conventions. No part of this book may be reproduced in any manner whatsoever without written permission from the publisher, except in the case of brief quotations embodied in critical articles and reviews.

ACKNOWLEDGMENTS

Bat City Review—"Soot" (winner of *Bat City Review*'s Editors' Prize)
Iron Horse Literary Review—"Sweet Corn"
Ninth Letter—"Red-Winged Blackbird"
Crab Orchard Review—"A Dream of Fish"
The Paris-American—"Learning To Curse"
TINGE Magazine—"Against The Wind"
Hayden's Ferry Review—"Portage, Indiana," "Certain Punishments"
The Portland Review—"Winter Poem With A Family"
Gulf Stream Literary Magazine—"Shaking Half-Beliefs"
Beecher's Magazine—"After My Father's Suicide"
Prairie Gold: An Anthology of The American Heartland—"Orchard"
Natural Bridge—"Summer Almanac"
The Broken Plate—"Posey County"
Hobart—"Having Been Called Dirt"

Publisher: Leah Huete de Maines
Editor: Christen Kincaid
Author Photo: Joe Betz
Cover Design: Elizabeth Maines McCleavy

Order online: www.finishinglinepress.com
also available on amazon.com

Author inquiries and mail orders:
Finishing Line Press
PO Box 1626
Georgetown, Kentucky 40324
USA

Table of Contents

Soot 1

Portage, Indiana 3

Learning to Curse 4

Red-Winged Blackbird 5

Against the Wind 6

Winter Poem With a Family 7

Knuckle Up 8

Sweet Corn 9

A Bright Afternoon to Conjure Spring, So I Try 10

After My Father's Suicide 11

Posey County 12

Summer Almanac 13

Shaking Half-Beliefs 15

A Dream of Fish 16

Certain Punishments 17

Orchard 18

Having Been Called Dirt 20

Farmer Suicide Wherein a Proclamation on Parenting Enters 22

A Guided Tour Through the Museum of Moments
    of Tenderness 25

With Thanks 28

SOOT

I walked into the living room
the way crabs on PBS navigate themselves against rocks
so my father said stop moving and sit down.

//

Wind pulled the dried hangnails of leaves
from limbs before depositing each
into the thickening river.

//

I imagined a fan circling above our heads like confused weathervanes
though the trailer had none but the box near the kitchen window
murmuring like a new and crag-pocked heart.

//

Ribs thinning
like a promise repeated, breath,
my father's bright cough through ash
blue teeth.

//

Twitch in the neck
emblem of methamphetamine's pulse:
cat's claw hooked in the eye's soft skin.

//

When he told me how the weather meant fire
in a coffee can's cup I saw two cardinals clutched
inside a tailpipe's vice.

//

Smoke bloomed against the ceiling as a new dark wound.
By Christmas our skin could be cleaned with a comb.

PORTAGE, INDIANA

Perfectly packaged boxes sit in the shadows of the shoe store
while a man pulls down the protective metal grating, giving me a
    goodnight,
the specials and discounts for men. I want to say something profound
but have my fists deep in coat pockets and can't make the appropriate
    gestures.

A woman passes me bundled in scarves. I remember my mother in
    snow boots
black and waxed with salt and tar from the potholed road that led to
    our door,
the house squatting into soil dark and rich with worms I'd pull from
    holes
in the basement walls, frozen, not ready to be pinched by fishing
    hooks I cleaned

religiously as guns my father kept. She was holding a cat and crying.
    It thawed
in the sink like a package of pulled pork left over from October.
Who knows where she found it. She would sometimes walk for hours.

LEARNING TO CURSE

If not for hopscotch
I might still be lost
in the parceled woods
of southern Indiana,
but the blacktop called
like cardinals flushed
from elderberry bushes,
that yip of dangerous
surprise, when your
own one-legged
flight was enough
to convince you
gravity *was* broken here,
apples fixed, sickening green,
in the trees half-shading
the basketball court, forever.
And today I think of them
bunched in knots, imagine
my arms, long enough now
to cuff the lowest limbs
and test stems that remain,
even in dreams, invisible,
and the memory of boys
older than me with wrists
thick as my neck, punching
the basketball into a confusion
of leaves to break our story,
until giving up, done,
they said, with our bullshit.

RED-WINGED BLACKBIRD

On corn tassels, dew. On our jeans, dew.
From his lips a boy wipes sweat thick
as pickling salt. Today no one is resting,
not even the sun high and burning like
a cross in misanthropic minds. On the radio,
love. On our minds, love. In the field
we're slipping wet hands in corn until we
walk slow as clouds plumping west to the
farmer asleep in his truck, rocks and lunch
boxes behind our burnt backs red as apples
now cooling to peel. No one is resting.
Our plan to bang these rocks, whip these
boxes for wild music, we slink. We are
children; mustard weed on pant legs.
And in fifteen feet, we will later say we knew
an engine's backfire did not ring but popped
to nothing, and in fifteen feet, we will
later say the sound was not the tractor's
basket clipping another well. We are children.
We smell him first. And in the early afternoon,
if you watch, a red-winged blackbird will
sit on a phone line for you silent
as waving hands, a plane in the sky.

AGAINST THE WIND

Small as deer ticks sequestered in ear hair
undiscovered through November,
as blood in dimples of wedding bands
sitting on bathroom sinks. How the wind
makes me. Coyote curling above bean hills,
alfalfa seed. Still the cardinal's red body
held in a cat's maw below the porch. Sunset.
Tonight I'll believe in good things.

                                              Cardinals flying.

WINTER POEM WITH A FAMILY

She passes venison on wooden plates
and uncles reach for their harmonicas.

Outside coyotes cry and jump
below a carcass hung in the pine tree.

At the table there is discussion of war in hushed tones
while the children go to their room.

They put on a puppet show with dolls
made of straw and old teeth from the workhorse.

It contains a man and a woman in love on a farm,
their families around a long table.

There is dancing and dancing, hees and haws.
Much clapping at the end with full bellies, and later

they will wash the plates, careful to keep the broken bones
for an idea of a show with an army.

KNUCKLE UP

Fists dense with nickel rolls,
two-dollar punches, we
swing heavy through new fog
built with sugar-sick breath.
Dangerous, flexing over every
reflective surface, new gods birthed
by mistimed pullouts, we preen. Pleasure

is the hook dense as cold molasses
through the interstice of two ribs,
coughed. // These performative
combos construct Sunday, affect worlds
built of ripped linoleum skin

stitched and buffed on the fifteenth
of next month, 32nd of
never   //   If you miss, if
you miss, if you miss //
stuttered prophecies of retribution
hiss between laughs serious as butter

absent the refrigerator, as chapped
lips' preemptive bleeding when smiles
stretch seasonal lessons regarding overindulgence
//   sting. We watch each punch
wind up like promise,
trading false haymakers in sync,
inexhaustible, pumpjacks lapping oil.

SWEET CORN

Subtle, the scent nudging past leaf
and stalk, dirt dry as knuckles washed
with gasoline, they tempted patience,
husk down flashing white
and yellow seeds, skin swelling
almost phosphorescent under sun
loud as the bullet to end a cow
turning itself in a barbwire vice.

//

I'd picked each ear heavy above my head
beading dew grasshoppers sipped
before spinning off in a buzz of legs,
my hands heavy with sleep
punch-drunk as wasps escaping Stroh's cans
filling a basket on my back. Coyotes turned
in hollow logs near the river.
Silence punctuated each step left.

//

Later no cars would stop. The sign
on which I'd written SALE
fell over in a semi's wake.
I dreamt of butter and salt, the good
hard plates, and counted corn snakes
writing my name across the highway.
When the farmer stopped
asking where I'd grown that corn
I felt the sun pull water from my neck,
knew my legs were faster than his mouth.

A BRIGHT AFTERNOON TO CONJURE SPRING, SO I TRY

Let me tell you about the underground hives of bumblebees below the oak tree. In spring you might think the tree talks. In spring you might think the tingle in your heel is precursor, some latent tendon warning you to stop. Nah. It's the bees. So walk to the garden, set the cucumber seeds below wire you've salvaged from busted shopping carts. Cast tomato seeds without worry, for the soil is good here and will take whatever you offer, greedily. Just look at the starts scattered around that plum tree. An extending ring of offspring lapping light. Dig some of those later and wrap roots in wet newspaper to offer neighbors. Can you hear those bees now? They're hungry. You're hungry. Believe no one who says we've nothing to learn from a bee's dance, a bird's call. Believe no one who says they've learned a bee's dance means please; a bird's call means *run*. Animals don't know our sirens but these bees ring like one today, my ear close to the ground, cheekbones rubbing roots impatient with dirt. I'm opening my mouth to sing a song for spring. I'm pretending I'm a small god whose voice matters to this space, these bees rising around me like a blanket stitching itself together, like promises written in yellow-black ink.

AFTER MY FATHER'S SUICIDE

Sometimes a willow tree
seeks a sewer pipe
large enough for a person
to stand inside.

                         And that grows, of course
                         that grows, until
                         stuck, dense as cold
                         fists in coat pockets

Sometimes the roots coil
like an idea on the glass
of a door you're asked
not to touch.

                         a man, flashlight-headed,
                         opens with an axe,
                         chainsaw, controlled burn
                         in the root's center

And they grow, of course
they grow, fed by the rush
of toilets and rain,
storm surges that lift houses.

                         he will scoop slowly
                         like wet ice cream
                         into a black bucket
                         for another to remove.

POSEY COUNTY

Red house
in the distance,
you are only
        red when
on fire, and today you
burn. Even
the crows
are happy
        on days like these.
The children
        and their dusty kites
have come from miles away,
playing
        in this swooping heat
that rises in drafts and is enjoyed
for as long as it lasts.

SUMMER ALMANAC

The fire ants split between the cracks
of the newly cemented porch, reappearing

like pocket knives clipping across
the metal bars found along the Kirk

Bridge, added after too many falls.
So it's red summer. So it's scorched earth lawns

and divorced family picnics covered in a gloss
of smiles. Almanac Advice: If bitten by an ant

note its size and color. If bitten by a snake,
catch it and note the fangs. My fingers

hang and drag against the cement below
the low swing. I guess at the time it would take

for them to bleed, knowing everything we touch
leaves a mark, like the telescope makers

taking thumbs to lenses to remove microscopic
pieces, and the wait after for the glass to cool

before more adjustments. The worries of a crack,
of ruin. The worries of adults that don't exist

in children, and the way we drink to find that again.
Tonight, I could tell you I've watched my hand swell

with ant bites and the stories of friends who jumped
screaming into lakes, their feet and calves covered

like over-iced cakes. The camping trips
and military tents. I could tell you it's humid

and snakes rest in the ditch shade like katydids
and just as numerous, all waiting for the motors

of push mowers to make the grass swim in a line
toward the water beyond the fence, but you want

to know about the fountains, so I'll tell you
the neighbor has found the outdoor socket

and the green ceramic glistens, drawing birds,
and tonight again mosquitoes will birth thousands there

in the still pools at its base. Almanac Advice: If bitten
by a spider, remove the bed sheets. If bitten by the sun, sleep only

with the top sheet. Tonight, I raise my glasses of beer
to the invisible face of happiness, then the dangerous

face of health with all its proof in scars and smiles
as the water calls an incessant yes. There is no place for this

to end, so the swing continues its slight arc and the sun
sets against my neck; my shadow is anything you want.

SHAKING HALF-BELIEFS

>   You stopped breathing
>   so I shot

>   hand on chest to test my anxious
> nature, and you lifted it, slightly,
> meaning *yes I'm alive*
> *yes I'm sleeping and*
> *yes, goddammit, I will wake*
>   *when I please,* all of it dotted

>   clear as brail in beards
> of Santa Claus pajamas
> which zip haphazardly from the calf
> which I picked specially from the shelf
> marked 3 months
> holding them to the light half-

>   believing you won't be

>   this big,   half-believing the time

> it's taken to write this means

>   you might be dead,

>   but now I push past half-
> beliefs to something true
> as table wood red-lacquered to shine
> in lamp light, as your mother's shape,
> soft step,

>   questioning pause

> in the hallway, as eyes
>   asking if you're alive

>   and I shake my head yes

> and she shakes her hips yes.

A DREAM OF FISH

Vestige of moon glow, lily pads on the Fisher's pond
in a town of fishermen and fisherwomen. I've known
nothing but the Ohio River and corn leaf cuts
thick as jam, nothing of villages rimmed
with salt, silt. Still, one dreams of nets

both filled with fish and also *swish*
for I was born of the trailer park's dirt
basketball court rimmed by blue grass,
the smell of cheap catfish fillets
helping to lift an under-pumped rubber ball.

Tonight, not far from that place, I gut
my family's meal with chagrin, a bottom-feeding
hoss tricked by dough balls and pig's blood,
smell rich with the nostalgic arch
of inevitability,
                        swimming the ceiling.

CERTAIN PUNISHMENTS

Broken lights cut the fingers of the curious boy, holding chalk.
Inside his school desk a mouse is dead inside a box
of matches. His teacher smokes at her desk and today
wears a red dress; she is the eternal hallway
in hell where no one can be late because they are already there.

Already the cut is drying and he is feeling better,
wanting soup, or the equivalent warmth, weather

or hearth conditioned. A man passes by, screaming for all to sign
his petition to end milk in schools; a dry bush catches fire and talks
in the language of bushes, outside and cold. Flocks
of geese fly in V's into uncounted ponds behind the Smith Cheese
Farm, home of the Equivalent Slice, and the packaging label: Buy,
     Please.

The boy writes numbers along a wall;
this is also, though conditioned, a type of fall.

ORCHARD
Bloomington, IN

1

On the bench I read,
mouth full of apple,
poets with dead fathers
should not write them
in or out of poems,
that an image of wasps
leaving a broken peach
left rotting on concrete steps
connotes so much pain,
and it's always pain,
that even descriptive suicides
shuck their skin
into the pathetic ditch.

2

In the orchard, bees
flying above their hive, the starts
from last year's strawberry patch
lifting white blossoms below peach
and apple trees. Four years old,
espalier training limbs to wire
like a yearly tailored smock,
buds promise fruit
that if left alone
might grow fat and fall
of its own volition, become part
of the soil, darkened by ants in waves.

3

And wasps, too, might be there,
but only because the sweet rot
calls their congregation,
and you'll notice they sing louder leaving
than arriving, their swoop before
skeptical and lovesick, as if they weren't
sure how to act before clenching mouthfuls,
in love with fall, the wrong idea of harvest.

HAVING BEEN CALLED DIRT

the water's instant when still
to stagnant, when mosquito larvae pops
into the toad's pink throat beneath sky
and super moon

//

an ember erupts the leaf pile
smoke as if a gun's barrel as if

//

escape the crack spreading air
stitching o's in boom

//

my father shot meth in the bathroom
brushed teeth with his left hand
loved me

//

the moment hand becomes fist as if
knuckles might matter as if
knowledge of a wall's stud as if

//

barn swallows cut the air
drunk with deer blood

//

i'm spinning circles in the graveyard
lost as last fall's breath kissing oaks
rolling birch bark tender my mind's fire
in a dog star cold as a sip of pond water

//

as if dirt was anything but
as if dirt was anything more

//

coyotes in the ribs of coyotes

FARMER SUICIDE WHEREIN A PROCLAMATION ON PARENTING ENTERS

> *A study by the Centers for Disease Control and Prevention (CDC) suggested that male farmers in 17 states took their lives at a rate two times higher than the general population in 2012 and 1.5 times higher in 2015. - The Guardian*

The farmer puts
the shotgun in
his mouth.
No one knows

if he let the barrel
sit on teeth or folded
lip. He'd already taken
the right boot

off, and it's
an arthritic bone's
task to save
the skull.

Have you listened
to the stomach
surreptitiously accept
its fate of cold

water? More
than babies
coo. More likely you
are listening

to the soft sound
of a curtain's
disintegration, the brown
bag of a mysterious

condition forcing
your elbow
to buckle. I've seen
a cow's brain

fried golden brown,
false blue
between pretzel buns.
I've retraced inches

of my daughter's spine
unbelieving the genome's
confidence to keep her crawling
through the arch of my body.

I've tossed my
daughter in the air
high enough to curse
God for her

laugh, how she
desires to go farther,
as I desire
to become tremor-

less, fear-
less of my ripped
shoulder, cracked
ribs. How I'd

break them again
if she said,   *for me.*
How I'd break you
if she said,   *they did.*

For the violence
inherent in a parent's hand
unfurls like a seed
when gifted combinations

of sunlight, water, and time.
O how it feeds
the conjured face. O how it feeds.
O how I cannot stop the morning.

A GUIDED TOUR THROUGH THE MUSEUM OF MOMENTS OF TENDERNESS

The only cassette tape slips into its slot.
Headphones uncoil a ragged cord pocked
with electrical tape and I'm touching
the play and fast forward options
like a toddler tracing the first letter
of their name with their whole hand.

//

A pamphlet instructs to begin
when entering Room 1,
to ignore the static, pops
like gravel to your house,
the impossibility
of stop.

//

Room 1's walls are the white of almost recall. A desk
in the middle. Two boys sharing it:
One whose head flickers off and on;
One whose belly flickers on and off. They hold
hands until a voice calls *stop* and the lights go out.
My mother's piano music.

//

The tape says *do not adjust the volume.*
The tape says *you will be feeling hot now.*
walk.
The doorway between rooms
drops the voice of my dead
great uncle Nathan calling me

//

kadiddlehopper kadiddlehopper
and the laughter after brightens
then dims the lights in Room 2.
Fresh hay. A room of fresh hay.
continue. through it. *note*
the soft itch of it.

//

The exit leads to a hallway.
On each side a bed extends from the wall.
Repeats beyond vision. Room enough
to walk, hands hovering
over each sheet the tape explains
was made for me *to sleep comfortably*

//

and the wind arriving now
is your father's breath on your forehead.
The first EXIT sign is false,
a cardboard box cut with kitchen scissors.
walk.
you are getting tired now. I want
to lay down. *walk. easy.*
Piano music.

//

The second EXIT sign
I don't notice
as the tape *explains*
you must exit, your

feet will blister, knees unhinge
like a double-jointed trick
that is no illusion. stop.

//

But I'm closer to an end.
The sheets do not appear to repeat
when the tape says
the sheets will repeat. they will.
they will. do not adjust the volume.

How long can I almost touch something

                                           without touching it?

With Thanks

Thank you, sincerely, to all editors and readers who believed in the poems above and thank you to Finishing Line Press for allowing me to join the many writers I admire who have come before me with this Press. Thank you, most importantly, to my family and friends who have encouraged, laughed, cried, and celebrated with me over these many years. I take nothing and no one for granted; I miss you all, and when you read this, know I am thinking of you, I can't wait to see you, and if we play some basketball, I'll let you take the first shot.

Joe Betz lives in Bloomington, IN with his wife, Megan, and daughter, Madeline. He is an Associate Professor of English at Ivy Tech-Bloomington. He has received awards for his poetry from *Michigan Quarterly Review* (Goldstein Prize), *Bat City Review* (Editors' Prize), and the University of Missouri–St. Louis (James Russell Grant Poetry Prize), where he earned his MFA in Creative Writing.

www.ingramcontent.com/pod-product-compliance
Lightning Source LLC
Chambersburg PA
CBHW022127090426
42743CB00008B/1043